T0317184

AN ANTHOLOGY OF

ROMANIAN WOMEN POETS

CLASSICS OF ROMANIAN LITERATURE
VOLUME VII

AN ANTHOLOGY OF

ROMANIAN WOMEN POETS

Edited by Adam J. Sorkin and Kurt W. Treptow

Illustrated by Ioana Lupuşoru

EAST EUROPEAN MONOGRAPHS
In cooperation with the
ROMANIAN CULTURAL FOUNDATION PUBLISHING HOUSE
DISTRIBUTED BY COLUMBIA UNIVERSITY PRESS
New York
1994

EAST EUROPEAN MONOGRAPHS, NO. CCCXCVII

CONTENTS

PREFACE

Poetry has always been an essential aspect of cultural expression in Romania, and this is no less true today than it was one hundred years ago. One will find few other countries where poetry has been such a force both culturally and politically. The effort to translate this poetry is an attempt to reveal something of the soul and the spirit of the people. To be culturally literate one must be acquainted with poetry, in addition to novels and stories; thus the idea of bringing forth in English translation the verse of some of the most significant Romanian women poets of the nineteenth and twentieth centuries takes on added significance.

This seventh volume in the series *Classics of Romanian Literature* fills an important gap as it is the first attempt to present systematically some of the most important Romanian women poets of the past two centuries. For too long their contribution has been underappreciated. This anthology is an effort to correct this oversight and to make their work known to an international audience.

By no means is this collection complete, and we readily recognize that many important names have been left out, such as Otilia Cazimir, Nina Cassian, Liliana Ursu, Denisa Comănescu, Ioana Ieronim, and Magda Cârneci, among others. This should not be interpreted to mean that we do not consider their contributions to Romanian literature to be equal to or greater than that of the poets presented in this anthology. Rather, the selection was made so as to represent different generations of Romanian Women poets, beginning with Veronica Micle and Matilda Cugler-Poni in the nineteenth century, through the inter-war period, represented most notably by Magda Isanos, to such important contemporary poets as Ana Blandiana and Daniela Crăsnaru, and even some younger, lesser known poets who merit attention and whose influence will grow in the years to come, such as Carmen Firan and Carmen Veronica Steiciuc. Indeed, the selection is somewhat subjective, being also dictated by the personal tastes and interests of the translators who worked on this anthology. Nevertheless, we believe the present volume gives the reader a good representative sample of many of the finest Romanian women poets of the past 150 years.

*****

There are many people who helped to make this anthology possible. We would like to thank Ioana Lupuşoru for her illustrations and for her enthusiastic support of the project from its very beginnings. In addition, we would also like to thank all of those who worked on the translations contained in this volume, and certainly the poets themselves. Without the efforts of these people this collection would not have been realized. The editors also wish to acknowledge grants they received from the Fulbright Scholar Program, with funds provided by the United States Information Agency (USIA), and the International Research and Exchanges Board (IREX), with funds provided by USIA, the National Endowment for the Humanities, and the Ford Foundation. Finally, we would like to express our sincere gratitude to Stephen Fischer-Galaţi for his support and commitment to the *Classics of Romanian Literature* project that he has made part of the *East European Monographs* collection.

The Editors

AN ANTHOLOGY OF

ROMANIAN WOMEN POETS

With translations by

Adam J. Sorkin, Kurt W. Treptow, Liviu Bleoca, Irina Andone, Andrei
Bantaş, Dan Duţescu, Laura Chistruga, Rodica Albu, Ioana Ieronim,
Maria-Ana Tupan, Sergiu Celac, Mia Nazarie, Angela Jianu,
and Ioana Lupuşoru

VERONICA MICLE
(1850-1889)

Quite unfairly, Veronica Micle is better known for having been the great love of Mihai Eminescu, Romania's national poet, than for having been one of the first significant Romanian women poets. She was born as Ana Cîmpan on 22 April 1850 at Năsăud in northern Transylvania, a region that provided some of the greatest names in Romanian literature, such as George Coşbuc (a well-known poet and brilliant translator) and Liviu Rebreanu (one of the greatest Romanian novelists).

Her father, who in 1848, under the command of the great Romanian patriot Avram Iancu, had fought against Hungarian efforts to annex Transylvania, died before the birth of his second child because of the wounds he received in battle. Soon his young widow moved to northern Moldavia with her two small children. After beginning primary school in Iaşi, the future poet changed her name from Ana to Veronica. After finishing the gymnasium in Iaşi, although only 14, she married a university professor named Ştefan Micle, with whom she had two daughters.

Veronica Micle first met Mihai Eminescu during a visit to Vienna in 1872. As a poet herself, she was quite aware of Eminescu's genius and deeply impressed by the man who would later be known as the "Hyperion of Romanian poetry." Their relationship began as an intellectual one, but soon became one of the most famous love stories in the history of Romanian literature. Their relationship, both before and after the death of Ştefan Micle in 1879, was tense and contradictory on a personal level, but deep and fruitful in terms of poetry. They had a strong impact on each other's literary activity. She inspired many of his most wonderful love poems, while he helped Micle to publish her only volume of poetry. Although they were deeply in love with one another, friends as well as enemies did their utmost to prevent the couple from getting married.

Though she published only a single volume of poems, Veronica Micle contributed verse to some of the most important literary magazines of the times such as *Convorbiri literare, Familia, Literatorul,* and *Revista nouă.* Her poetry includes love poems as well as descriptive ones, poems dedicated to friends, and poems to her daughters. Although much less profound than Eminescu's writings, her literary work is full of sentiment and indicative of different stages of their destiny. Some of her poems can be considered as a sort of lyrical diary, providing the psychological background or simply revealing details of her relationship with Eminescu. For instance, "If I Could Reach Out" was written in 1883 after she learned that Eminescu's mental illness had worsened.

Veronica Micle committed suicide at the Văratic Monastery, near Târgu Neamţ, less than two months after Eminescu's death, on 3 August 1889. Her houses, both in Târgu Neamţ and at the Văratic Monastery are museums that can be visited today. Like her entire life, her poetry was deeply influenced by him, and yet one can always find a freshness and sincerity that is all her own.

Liviu Bleoca

YOU, FAIR, SACRED POETRY
[*Frumoasă, sfântă poezie*]

You, fair, sacred poetry,
The only God I ever knew,
Your most enchanting vanity
My soul has valued most in you.

Yet so important did I feel
For having chosen you to suit
My striving for an idol. With a will
I've often paid you my tribute.

My very deepest piety
And your myth have made a whole,
So to your sweetest vanity
I've offered freely my own soul.

Translated by Liviu Bleoca

THIS WIDE WORLD...
[*Lumea mare...*]

As this world, so wide and empty, at my feet,
unbounded lies,
I do not try to embrace it with my mind or with my eyes;
And within this endless chaos, without any sense at all,
You have given, my sweet darling, shelter to my poor soul.
Therefore, my dearest one, when I sometimes think of you,
I see that the love I feel, like this world, is boundless too.

Translated by Liviu Bleoca

ONCE YOU WERE TO ME SO DEAR
[*Drag mi-ai fost...*]

Once you were to me so dear,
But what is done can't be undone,
I have seen this world is not
Empty without you, dear one.

Thus, too, Lucifer on high,
Praised for shining there so bright,
Will go down and disappear
Once the sun darts forth his light.

He with his so glorious disc
Flings the door of life ajar,
Makes you easily forgetful
Of the fading morning star.

Once bright Lucifer to me
Splendid in your daybreak glitter,
You've set — now I watch the sun
With a longing so much sweeter.

Translated by Liviu Bleoca

IF I COULD REACH OUT...
[Să pot întinde mâna...]

If I could reach out slowly, my hand if I could lay
So gently on your forehead, I'd draw your locks away
To keep your brow untroubled, and pure lily-white,
Beloved, sacred icon I worship day and night.

But in my life you're like the distant morning star
That only now and then will twinkle from afar;
And then you disappear for good leaving behind
The image that I worship forever in my mind.

Translated by Liviu Bleoca

THAT NOW...
[*Că astăzi*]

That now I am no longer master
Over my soul, and over me,
I've told you quite enough with just a
Squeeze of hand, so silently.

And that I am a poor plaything
In your mighty hand today,
My eyes, to you, would now be speaking
If only you did look this way.

And that I have but one desire,
To be your slave until I die,
Says my whole self you set on fire
Whenever you are passing by.

And yet, you pass more like the beam
The sun would on a beggar throw —
What does it care that it falls on him...
What do you care that I love you so!

Translated by Liviu Bleoca

MATILDA CUGLER-PONI
(1851-1931)

Like Veronica Micle, Matilda Cugler-Poni is one of many poets who began her career as a writer in the *Junimea* literary circle. Born in Iaşi on 2 April 1851, she lived in her native city most of her life, making intermittent trips to Paris, playing an active role in the literary life of the time, especially within the context of *Junimea*. She published her first poem in the literary magazine of the society, *Convorbiri literare*, when she was only sixteen. The daughter of an Austrian architect, Carl von Cugler, who had settled in Romania, the poet was educated in French, German, Italian, and Romanian literature. She later married the famous Romanian chemist Petru Poni. Her literary work is comprised mainly of poetry, together with a few sketches and short stories with realistic accents and a comedy. Most of her writings were first published in the literary magazines of the times, then later collected in volumes; her first volume of poems was published in Iaşi in 1874, while a second edition appeared in Bucharest in 1885. Her comedy, *A Tutor*, proved to be a success and was performed in Transylvania by various amateur theatrical companies.

Cugler-Poni's verse was very much appreciated in the *Junimea* circle for its *"elegance of style"* and *"sincerity of feeling"* (Titu Maiorescu). The famous Romanian historian A.D. Xenopol ranks among her most enthusiastic admirers. Her poems reminded her contemporaries of Heine and Lenau, with their specific *Weltschmerz*; the 19th century Romanian reader was very receptive to this type of sensibility. Yet for the modern reader much of the verse from her youth seems naive and conventional, sometimes including a moral lesson. Nevertheless, her work is not absent of poetic achievements. Varying in structure and poetic meaning, her verse is fluent and the poet sometimes frees herself from sentimentality and from the exterior, rhetorical tone, becoming "objective," distilling her feelings through the filter of folklore and, when her lyricism is concentrated, in short, well-balanced poems. The predominant theme in Cugler-Poni's writings is love. Her verse is sometimes exuberant, glorifying "the most beloved...," while at other times it expresses the calm after the tempest of unfulfilled passion. There are also the moments of serenity of an imparted love ("O, keep quiet and let time elapse"). A certain "sweet sorrow" pervades many of her poems ("He slowly advanced toward me"), but this is by no means the only tone to be found in Matilda Cugler-Poni's poetry. Some short epic poems are inspired by images drawn from Romanian folklore, while others deal with elementary forms of sensibility, recounting love and death with a vigorous accent. The same vitality and dynamic resources of her language can be found in her poems dealing with social themes, especially recounting the harsh life of the peasants. She died in Iași, at the age of 80, on 9 September 1931. The poems presented in this anthology reveal only some aspects of this complex writer, one of the first significant Romanian women poets.

Irina Andone

HE SLOWLY ADVANCED TOWARD ME
[*****]

He slowly advanced toward me
And my hand did he touch,
And then I his deep eyes
Did scrutinize.

What did I see in them?
O, nobody will find,
As all my grief and longing
Was lying there, inside.

Translated by Irina Andone

O, KEEP QUIET...
[*****]

O, keep quiet and let time elapse
Like the water that flows in the valley,
Both mirroring all on its shores
And never suspending its course.

Let my head find its rest
On your chest, in sweet peace,
'Cause the greatest of all happiness
Is the happiness that silent keeps.

Translated by Irina Andone

THE TRAVELER
[*Călătorul*]

Away, so faraway from his beloved place,
On paths never before stepped on by man's foot,
With broken heart and distress on his face,
Pale and silent climbs a traveler with no root.

From time to time, he wipes a tear, stopping,
Stretches an arm as if to catch a face's call,
Then deeply sobs and on his path keeps going
With lowered brow in tiring stroll.

What kind of woe torments him in his soul?
His sweetheart has he left on a distant shore?
Or is it that his mother is longing for him, sole,
While, by his fate exiled, he's leaving nowhere for?

With sadness the flowers look at him as he walks,
The zephyr with inquiring whispers talks:
`What much desired message and what sweet demand
Am I to bring to people much beloved?'

The traveler gives no answer, but cries and moves along.
O, full of pity, flowers, if you could know his grief
You'd wither all with sorrow, and you, the zephyr sweet,
Would change into cold tempest, thrilled.

He no longer has a mother, he no longer has a brother,
Alone he passed through life, an orphan as no other.

He only had a dear one, in her all things he found
And, once again, with her, all into darkness drowned.

He loved her so! But, on a mournful day,
Death's pale angel saw her in his way.
So beautiful and mild she was! And under such delight
To happiness' land he took her in his flight.

Alone then he remained and uncomforted,
Deprived of hope, with no god in his heaven.
O, do not urge him, zephyr, to tell you all his woe —
His way is dark, in peace so let him go!

Because there are no greater and everlasting tortures
Than those his doleful chest do stir:
He knows that none is waiting, none crying
and none longing for the sad traveler.

Translated by Irina Andone

THE MOST BELOVED KING
[*Regele cel mai iubit*]

Sometimes I am overwhelmed
By the most fantastic dreams,
As if my soul's in flames,
And my heart awakes, it seems.

You can't know then what a power,
What a strength I feel inside me,
It's as if I could, at will,
Crush the whole world in an hour.

If I would like, another earth,
Sun and moon I could rebuild,
And the crown of this whole world
On your brow would sit.

You would be this kingdom's king
And your people I would be,
Your desires would be commands,
With much love fulfilled to thee.

On the hillocks full of green,
There, your throne would be ascended,
And made up of living flowers
Your wreath would be resplendent.

Glory and fame you wouldn't have,
Crowds wouldn't kneel at your word,
But you'd be in all this world
The most belovéd king.

Translated by Irina Andone

PEASANTS IN THE CITY
[*Ţăranii în oraş*]

Boyars, to you we have been sent
by the people of our village
My brother and I, so chosen went
To say that we have cried

For land, but all in vain
And in desperate want
Tormented and no one deign
to know our plight or hear our plead

Great boyars, we are starving!
And our cattle are growing thin
Having neither grass nor bushes dying
As only barren ground they eat

Even God has punished us, every one,
For such a time it hasn't rained!...
Burned and parched by the sun
Stay the fields that we have worked.

As for us, what will be, will be
But our poor children
Think of them at least! Look and see
How could you keep them

Hungry all day long?
When they ask, you've nothing to give them!...
Boyars, don't disappoint us or do us wrong
And God will not abandon you

God has given the land
Also for the poor
And for good and bad by his hand
The crops upon it grow

We the hungry, we work it
And for others are its crops
We irrigate it with our sweat
To feed the satiated

And it's not right!... We await
For you to give us a reply
For we also have our rights, emancipate
We, the workers of the land!

Translated by Kurt W. Treptow and Ioana Lupuşoru

CARMEN SYLVA
(1843-1916)

Carmen Sylva (Latin for "song of the forest") was the pen name of Princess Elizabeth von Wied, who later became Romania's first queen. She was born in Neuwied Castle, on the banks of the Rhine, on 29 December 1843. The father of the future queen, Hermann von Wied, was a philosopher and artist, while her mother, Maria von Nassau, displayed a fondness for music and literature. They would instill these interests in their daughter.

Princess Elizabeth received a thorough artistic education from early childhood. She studied the piano, vocal music, drawing, and painting. When only 15 she read Ovid, Cicero, and Horace, which enhanced her interest in literature. Gifted with languages, Princess Elizabeth was fluent in English, French, Italian, Russian, Swedish, and later Romanian, and she could read both Latin and Greek. While her father exposed her to the philosophical works of Kant, Fichte, and others, her mother took her on visits to hospitals and asylums.

Invited to Berlin by Queen Augusta of Prussia to complete her studies, she met Prince Carol von Hohenzollern-Sigmaringen, her future husband, who later became King Carol I of Romania. The couple married in 1869.

In 1866, Carol had been called upon by the Romanian government to become Prince of the Romanian Principalities (at that time, Wallachia and Moldavia) in an attempt to end the conflict between the rival Ghica and Studza families. He became the founder of modern Romania, laying the basis for modern European institutions in a country that had been under Turkish domination for centuries. In 1877 he led the war against the Turks that brought Romania its independence. In 1881, he was crowned King of Romania.

Princess (later Queen) Elizabeth was fully aware of the great responsibilities that lay with her and her husband. She introduced social assistance programs in Romania, and, due to her experience in charity work, she was able to help organize orphanages, schools for the blind, soup kitchens for the poor, etc. Fascinated by Romanian folk costumes, she made efforts to reinvigorate national home industries and organize exhibitions, and she published a book of Romanian folk costume patterns. She even introduced the folk costume as a gala dress for certain ceremonies at the royal court.

Meanwhile, her artistic activities never ceased. She was a prolific writer but also enjoyed drawing, painting, illustrating books, and doing artistic needlework. Carmen Sylva's literary and musical soirées at the Castle of Peleş in Sinaia or in Bucharest were famous. She often accompanied on the piano her protégé, George Enescu, violin player and Romania's greatest composer.

Carmen Sylva published some 50 books, 20 of which were volumes of poetry. She wrote novels, dramas, short stories, legends, and nursery rhymes. With few exceptions, she wrote most of her literary work in German. Among her translators into Romanian, the most important were Mihai Eminescu, George Coşbuc, and Octavian Goga. She in turn translated into German poems by Mihai Eminescu, Vasile Alecsandri, and Dimitrie Bolintineanu, as well as selections of Romanian folk poetry.

Queen Elizabeth died on 21 October 1916, two years after the death of her husband, King Carol I. Although not as great a writer as some of her contemporaries, Carmen Sylva ranks as one of Romania's most remarkable women writers and people of culture.

Liviu Bleoca

THE BLACK SAILING SHIP
[*Corabia neagră*]

As night closes in, a ship sails away,
The vaulted sails stir and rise to the sky,
On the troublesome waters she staggers her way
With a black mourning banner fluttering high.

The oars drag along this most precious load
As slaves could hardly carry their burdensome chain;
A vigorless tremor the oars gently goad
Like the long sound of convicts sighing in vain.

She floats on the waters, so lifeless and slow;
She glides like the shadow of someone long gone,
Fulfilling her fate: to sail or to row
From morning till night, from dusk to dawn.

On deck, by the bow, a pour soul is awake;
With locks flying wildly, a sad woman sighs
Near the stern, where angry waves break.
You can see despair and tears in her eyes.

But nobody knows why and wither they sail,
And late, in the distance, their image gets thin.
The vast sea disperses the ship's foamy trail,
And all fade away as night closes in.

Translated by Liviu Bleoca

SONNET
[*Sonet*]

O, come and listen to the merry song
Of birds that sing by scores in grove and plain:
So happy that the flowers rise again,
And that the wide world's splendid all along.

Do you think so? The birds sigh sadly all day long
When locked in some cage well fastened with a chain,
She sings, alas, her never-ending pain
To be a slave, not free. Again you're wrong!

O, no, I know she simply sings
Because for melodies her beak was meant,
No matter whether she is captive here or springs

Up through the hoary clouds, in spaces without end
She sings for she's a poet. The same force brings
And keeps the fire burning from heaven sent.

Translated by Liviu Bleoca

THE GRAVE DIGGER'S SONG
[*Cântecul groparului*]

I'd tap at her window with such gentle hand:
"My love, let me in, don't hasten my end,

Don't freeze with your heart the fire within.
My life, my good fortune, I pray, let me in."

The beauteous lady would come into sight.
She would help me in with arms soft and white.

No one ever knew the blessed days we had
United in secret, and now she is dead.

So I dug a bedding in yonder soft clay
For the smile that has passed forever away.

By night, to her room I'd sneak like a knave,
Now too, in the night, I was digging her grave,

So no one would learn in the dead of the night
Of her precious love — the tears that I fight.

Translated by Liviu Bleoca

PLOWING
[*La arat*]

Romanian land needs toilsome furrows, deep and neat,
Eight mighty oxen pull the yoke with heavy strife
From cool and early morn till evening heat,
Led by the white-clad peasant and his wife.

She urges on the oxen while he's busy pushing nigh,
They labor now to get the crop out of the earth's folds.
And when at night a thousand stars are scattered in the sky,
They leave barefoot and tired like the baby that she holds.

Translated by Liviu Bleoca

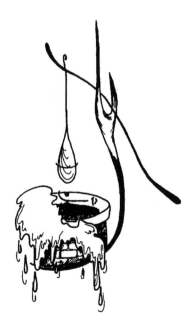

THREE FRIENDS
[*Trei tovarăși*]

We lived as dear friends, inseparable, free,
The ancient forest and the song and me,
And also our Rhine with banks so fair,
Oh, how we dreamt those nights alight with moon:
The forest softly sang, I played another tune,
And on its waves the Rhine a whispered song did bear.

But then my destiny was that I roam
Across the world, and build another home
Away from there, lost in foreign lands.
"It's hard to leave those that you love so true —
My dear friends, a farewell to you,
Or rather come with me, my dear friends!"

"We do love you," the forest answered back,
"But we are much too old to take the track,
And wander through the world along with you!"
The Rhine then said to me: "I've always flown
This way, so stay on these banks that you've known!
In yonder gloomy realms what will you do?"

So, finally, I left, O, poor me,
And by the Danube stopped eventually.
I am so far away from those so dear,
But as I stopped and looked around,
A smiling, dear friend I found.
Sweet song, you too have traveled here.

Translated by Liviu Bleoca

MAGDA ISANOS
(1916-1944)

Though her death at the tender age of 28 ended her literary career prematurely, Magda Isanos still ranks among the greatest Romanian poets of all time. Born in Iaşi on 17 April 1916 into a Romanian family that had emigrated from Transylvania to Moldavia some generations earlier, Magda was the first of five daughters of Mihai and Eliza Isanos. Both of her parents were doctors, having met while attending medical school in Iaşi. Following World War I and the reunification of Bessarabia with Romania after a long period of occupation by the Russian Empire that began in 1812, the family moved to Chişinău where the future poet grew up and attended school.

Magda Isanos began writing poems at an early age, making her debut in the student magazine *Licurici* in 1932 when only sixteen years old. This marked the beginning of a fruitful literary career as she began to publish poems in many of the major cultural journals of the time.

After finishing high school in Chişinău, Isanos returned to the city of her birth in 1934 to enter Law School at the University of Iaşi. She also took courses in philology and philosophy in keeping with her passion for literature and culture. During the inter-war period, Iaşi was the cultural capital of Romania and proved to be a vibrant and exciting environment for the young poet. She became active with a group of writers around the cultural magazine, *Însemnări ieşene*, originally founded by the famous poet and writer George Topîrceanu.

Following a brief, failed marriage, Isanos met a fellow writer, Eusebiu Camilar. The two fell in love and were married in Iaşi on 31 March 1939. The tragedy that accompanied the outbreak of the war later that same year, leading to the Soviet occupation of Bessarabia and northern Bucovina, and the Hungarian occupation of northern Transylvania in 1940, marred the lives of the young couple. Though appalled at the communist takeover of the region where she grew up, Isanos remained firm in her opposition to the war for humanitarian reasons. The poet's disdain for violence is reflected in several of her works. The miseries of war also helped aggravate her health problems; always frail, she suffered from a heart condition. Her infirmity accounts for the obsession with death that pervades many of her poems. It is as if the poet knew of her approaching end.

Nevertheless, the war years also brought Magda Isanos two of the greatest joys in her life, the birth of her only child, Elisabeta, and the publication of her first volume of poems, *Poezii* (Iaşi, 1943). Her literary activity continued throughout this whole period, as she wrote not only poems, but short stories and articles as well.

Forced to flee Iaşi in 1944 as the Soviet armies crossed the Dniester and later the Prut rivers into Romanian territory, the young couple took refuge in Bucharest. Tragedy struck on the night of 5-6 June 1944 when Soviet air bombardment decimated the poet's home in Iaşi, destroying many of her manuscripts. The frailty of the young poet was enhanced by the brutal Soviet occupation of the country following 23 August 1944 when Romania agreed to sign an armistice with the allies. This contributed in large measure to her death in Bucharest on 17 November 1944. Ironically, the promising literary career of Magda Isanos was cut short by the brutality of the war that she so much opposed.

Following her death, two posthumous volumes of her poems appeared, *Cântare munţilor* (1945), and *Ţara luminii* (1946). Together with her first book of poems, these volumes demonstrated a remarkable talent that helped to establish her as one of the leading Romanian poets of the twentieth century.

Kurt W. Treptow

THAT SKY
[*Cerul acela*]

That sky slowly fell down
with a blue fragrance, in my sight,
at that sad time when the stars shone
as some cups half-filled with light.

As eyes tired from a dream
the astral irises were blooming
and the last night cranes were soaring
dimly as in ponds I've seen.

It was dawn and quiet within frontiers
so that you could hear how the flower sings
like the angel's white rising wings
far away, in blameless spheres.

Translated by Laura Chistruga

THE ICON
[*Icoana*]

And the mother of God came. (A blue so fair
was her gown as in the icon.)
She took from the table a cup and moved on
to our left and gave a drink to a soldier there.

Then a seat further down she took,
with her head slightly bent.
Surrounded by a halo, as in a book,
she sat thoughtfully, intent.

I don't know who said to me:
"'tis but a dream you see."

Translated by Kurt W. Treptow

THE ANGELS
[*Îngerii*]

The angels arrived late in the night.
They sat watching in a row,
leaning on spears with golden points so bright.
Their thick wings suffocated us so.

"Did your angel come?" sometimes I'd ask.
Then suddenly I saw it shining,
at the legs of the bed, to the ceiling
in the light of its wings the room did bask.

They didn't sparkle: their sapphire shrouds,
old soldiers and peaceful crowds.
They were flying when morning came,
leaving a blue stripe on the window pane.

Translated by Kurt W. Treptow

OVER FUTURE FIELDS
[Peste câmpiile viitoare]

Over future fields
will shine brighter rainbows.
Songs and parties will be held
at the planting and harvest
of those fields.

Long live in glory, mountains high!
Praise
to the hands which seek to raise
up to your brilliant peaks, so far yet nigh!
Cornfields and hymns will harvest
the people of tomorrow.
They will praise the sun without sorrow
and they will sing as blest.

Over future fields will glow
the brilliant colors of the rainbow.
In golden meadows will
silver plows the soil till.

People, sing!
We are one: both serf and king.
The same quiet, gentle fate,
for those who rise and those who fall does await.

Translated by Kurt W. Treptow

IN THE FOREST
[*În pădure*]

In the spring forest I once saw
God pass by, his entourage in awe,
and impart to every bud a spark
as from a sapphire no longer dark.

The murmuring sap departs and becomes one
as it unites with rays from the shining sun;
one morning, after a snowfall,
even the leaves began to see it all.

Then everything appeared so bright,
full of dew and kissed by starlight,
in the night which held us for hours
like unblossomed and dormant flowers.

Translated by Kurt W. Treptow

NIGHT
[*Noapte*]

We listen this night
to the forest blooming, full of whispers trite,
as high as space so infinite,
the same and different;
with branches blossomed once again,
I no longer know from where they begin.
The darkness became thick as tar —
and cold around you, star...

Where are they now, where are they,
the beings, mysterious things reconciled,
near the ground like shadows piled
and smelling of earthen clay?

Translated by Kurt W. Treptow

DEAR GOD, I'VE NOT FINISHED YET!
[*Doamne, n-am isprăvit!*]

Dear God, I've not finished yet
the song you sang me when we met.
Don't send me angels of fire and ice
every evening, sometimes twice.

I cannot leave. The trees whisper to me so;
the flowers stand in my way and won't let me go.
About this I've started a song these days,
a poem of naive wonder and praise.

I wanted to leave for people my spirit
as bread at a wayside when they stop for a minute,
to be their pasture, orchard, and sky.

For all those with whom I have no tie
and don't know me, I desire
to be a votive light, pure fire.

I searched in the grass and clover
for secrets hidden from all. Moreover
I was looking in the well, the pond, and seas
and I was listening — endlessly — under the fir trees...

Then the angels came and called me.
Dear God, I can't leave, I've not finished! Don't you see!
Open the cage and put to flight
the impatient verses that fill my soul day and night.

Translated by Laura Chistruga and Kurt W. Treptow

I HAVE TO LEAVE THIS NIGHT
[*Trebuie să plec astă-seară*]

I have to leave this night
or tomorrow. An angel so very bright
will come to my bed and say:
get up, do not delay.

Dear angel, leave me in this world.
Leave your windy wings thus furled
and let your eyes see:
everything is blooming, why not also me?

Let me yet cast my shadow around,
on waving waters, on the ground,
to gather flowers and make a wreath...
I just ask more time to me bequeath.

Take a branch and create a woman,
bring her before God, a human;
innocent, my actions she'll defend
for my whole life up to the end.

Translated by Laura Chistruga and Kurt W. Treptow

I WISH FOR A FAIRY TALE
[Aş vrea un basm]

I wish for a fairy tale, but who'll tell me one
when even the wind's been silent for a time?
There's no fire in the hearth, and moonlight none,
and my good muse won't whisper any rhyme.

There was a girl and a grandpa, one day;
there were nice tales, red poppies in the field;
perfume and crickets singing in the hay —
but since then time has much revealed.

The old man is now dead, no word his lips can bear.
He's sleeping in his bed of good, old ground,
had he lived now, I wonder who would care
to listen to his wise advises, how they sound?

I hear the furniture, its sad, old sigh,
the wind seems to be crying at the door —
the tireless, short seconds quickly fly.
....
A fairy tale before sleep I hear no more.

Translated by Laura Chistruga and Kurt W. Treptow

WANDERING WITH THE MOON
[*Rătăcind cu luna*]

It's so nice to wander a whole night
carrying the moon, like an amphora, on your shoulder,
to feel, like over-ripened fruits in June — bright,
numerous thoughts in your disorder.

    The cobblestone lies like a silver water
    that slowly winds, luring your tired feet,
    the houses show their windows through
                which the quarter
    of the pale moon has tried in vain to fit.

Silver and honey flew over the park...
Maybe in this splendor it has made
— in a sweet drunkenness of white light and dark —
acacia flowers sing a fragrant serenade,

    and it is her, this splendor, that tonight
    makes your heart long for a true love word
    and for a time that passed and was so bright
    but now lies somewhere like a rusty sword.

Like the cold arm of a dead queen
is the moon, holding your shoulder —
Her, wandering ghost and you, her twin
trying to count thoughts coming in disorder.

Do stop, take your forehead in your hands,
and, if you have no choice, do cry.
'cause you will make the moonlight die
only by the hot sun when the night ends.

Translated by Laura Chistruga

[LIKE SOME LIGHT STEPS...]
[*Ca niște pași...*]

Like some light steps, like wings dipped in light
memories are touching my soul,
and charmed by this bright, shining flight,
clear as the autumn dawn, I feel whole.

Memories are sailing toward my heart
like ships returning from far away,
by their heavy burden nearly torn apart,
they bring me joys of love now gone astray.

Who knows, maybe you've sent them here,
so with their bewitched net they'd catch me
and through a portal of dreams bring me in your sphere,
the way a fisherman brings his catch from the sea.

Translated by Laura Chistruga and Kurt W. Treptow

MARIA BANUȘ
(1914-   )

A poet whose career has spanned both the inter-war period and the communist era, Maria Banuș was born in Bucharest on 10 April 1914. Taken with poetry at an early age, she made her literary debut at the tender age of fourteen. In 1937, the publication of her first volume of poems, *Țara fetelor*, created a sensation as her verses displayed a unique sensuality, vitality, and expressiveness rarely encountered up to that time.

Unfortunately, the great promise exhibited in her early writings was overshadowed by the political fate of Romania after World War II, as the country passed under Soviet domination and a communist regime was installed in Bucharest. Like many other intellectuals of her generation forced to choose between serving the political aims of the Stalinist regime or suffering in communist prisons, Maria Banuș, a Jewish intellectual and devout anti-fascist, chose the former. Her writings of the period after the Second World War reflect active support for the aims of the communist regime, and she was a devout believer that Marxism and socialism were necessary for the progress and happiness of Romanians. In poems such as "Aici s-a născut Stalin" ["Stalin was born here"] published in 1950 in the principal Romanian literary journal *Viața românească*, she unabashedly praised the Soviet dictator responsible for the deaths of thousands of Romanians. A further volume of poems published in 1955, *Ție-ți vorbesc, Americă*, blatantly served the communist regime's interests by attacking American imperialism in the world. These works helped tarnish Banuș's reputation.

Her later work turned away from politics and has again demonstrated the poetical talents that have made her one of the leading Romanian women poets of her generation, combining the vitality of the poetry of her youth with a remarkable simplicity and austerity. She has been a prolific writer, publishing numerous volumes of poetry during her lifetime. In addition to her poetry, Banuş has done many translations of great writers of world literature into Romanian. While her use of art to serve political interests, particularly during the 1950's, can be condemned, no one can deny that Maria Banuş has produced many remarkable poems that justify her being classified among the finest Romanian women poets. She is perhaps best seen as a representative figure of her generation.

Kurt W. Treptow

EIGHTEEN
[*Optsprezece ani*]

The streets are wet. It's been raining with drops round
                                                  and full
like silver coins that the sun had turned to gold.
My thought would charge at the world like a bull.
Today I'm eighteen years old.

The placid rain pelts me with many a crazy idea.
See, a slow drop trickles down from the warm shower
as when I was squeezed in my pram, I fear,
by wet diapers unchanged for an hour.

Yes, it's been raining like tomorrow and yesterday and
                                                  when not.
A heart is searching the times, the heart is one.
My temple throbs harder than time's fast trot.

I have a mind to take long sips of life like a bum,
but even the pungent steam of the broth burns me so.
Today I'm eighteen years old, you know.

Translated by Dan Duţescu

SONG TO ROCK THE KNEES
[Cîntec de legănat genunchii]

My knees don't cry out, my knees.
A path of night ferns and of rain.
How do those iron knees bend you?
I drive you to them like two lambs.

Along the hazy path I call out to you.

Maybe they'll take you between them
those throbbing, heavy, squeezing knees
that are like the night of astrakhan.
And glow worms of footsteps fade out.

My knees don't cry out, my knees.

Translated by Dan Duțescu

BETWEEN TWO RUINS
[*Între două ruine*]

Between two ruins I built a house,
between two treasons I planted a belief,
between two chasms I set a table with napkins
                              and salt shakers,
between mountains of corpses I saw a saffron
                              and I smiled at it.
That is how I lived. Can you understand now?
                  That is how I lived.

Translated by Dan Duţescu

WE WERE JUST LEAVING THE ARENA
[*Tocmai ieşeam din arenă*]

Just because you are so much younger than I am,
I want to teach you and say,
"Be daring," or "Be patient,"
"Be a fox," "Be a lion,"
as one usually says to those younger.
We were just leaving the arena, we were under the stars,
under the sky of the August sea,
and all the truths that in the arena
were strong, as substantial as precious ores,
had been pulverized into thousands of silvery drops
that wouldn't allow me to speak.

Translated by Dan Duțescu

ONCE, THE ANGEL OF DEATH
[*Odată, îngerul morţii*]

Once, the angel of death
came in the guise of a baker.
His clothes, his face, his hands
were all white with flour.
In his hand he carried a shovel.
From the oven a fragrance blew
of bread baked in the light.
His gestures were rhythmical, grave.
The wheel and the sun, the round loaf,
followed each other in unhurried rotation,
at the mouth of the oven,
in a beautiful, incessant rotation.

"Of you I'm not afraid, baker,
you look just like Iani
in the street of my childhood,
in the paradise of the pie shops."

This I was telling him
when he rose up toward me
a face that was hidden
in a hideous light.

Behind him there roared in fetters
the oven of holocausts,
and the good baker,
his apron powdered with flour,
the angel of death, of the sun,

revealed to my eyes
his sprawling, hollowed trunk,
with poisonous mushrooms
stuck to the roots.

Translated by Dan Duțescu

I SAY TO MY PEN
[*Spun creionului*]

I say to my pen,
"Take this way,
the grass is soft in the moonlight,
the leaves are singing like doves —
You damned slave!
I'm wasting my words on you!
Where are you going?
Into gray dismal courtyards with burned grass,
with livid dressings, under crushed rubble,
with garbage bins —
Where are you eavesdropping?
At the back window, the death rattle —
Go away, I tell you.
Nobody can help him.
Wretched slave, do you hear me?

Translated by Dan Duţescu

ILEANA MĂLĂNCIOIU
(1940-   )

Born into a peasant family in Godeni in the county of Argeş on 23 January 1940, Ileana Mălăncioiu attended the University of Bucharest, graduating with a degree in Philosophy in 1968. She completed her Ph.D in 1975. The subject of her doctoral dissertation was "Tragic Guilt," which in itself is significant for the outlook and essence of her poetry. She has had a wide range of cultural activities, at various times working for the Romanian Television, as an editor on the cultural journal *Argeş*, and at the Anima Film Studio. Presently she is the assistant editor in chief of the prestigious literary journal *Viaţa românească*.

Beginning with her first volume of poems *Pasărea tăiată*, published in 1967, Mălăncioiu has established herself as one of the major poets working in Romania today. In addition to her numerous volumes of poetry, she has also published several books of essays and criticism. Her book of poems, *Crini pentru domnişoara mireasă*, won the prize of the Romanian Academy in 1973. In 1985, Editura Eminescu in Bucharest published a dual language volume of 124 of Mălăncioiu's poems, *Peste zona interzisă/Across the Forbidden Zone*, translated by Dan Duțescu. Throughout her poetical work, she proves to be a fighter for humanity and against intolerance and dictatorship.

Dan Duțescu

THE SLAUGHTERED FOWL
[*Pasărea tăiată*]

The old folks have shut me up according to custom
So that I should not lose my memory because of the
                                        slaughtered fowl
And I listen through the bolted door
How it kicks and tosses about, a lost soul.

I twist the bolt weakened by time
Trying to forget what I heard, to get rid of the dread
Of this tossing about in which
The body is running after its head.

And I wince when the eyes, freezing in terror,
Roll up to show their white
They look like maize grains
And other fowl nibble at them and fight.

I take the head in one hand, the rest in the other
And I change hands when under the weight I sway
Before they die let them be tied together
Through my body, at least in this way,

The head however dies sooner
As if the killing hasn't been done properly maybe
And so that the body should not throb alone
I let the death flow into it through me.

Translated by Dan Duțescu

LILIES FOR HER LADY THE BRIDE
[Crini pentru domnişoara mireasă]

Lilies for her lady the bride
Lilies white and buxom never seen before
As if an eternal wedding had just been discovered
By a young bridegroom true to the core.

What do you carry, dear groom, in the bouquet of
                                    three flowers
In the bouquet of three divine faces
Like three lily flowers brought from far away
For the fairy tale wedding that it graces?

His lord, the bridegroom can make no answer
His lord, the bridegroom is flying over these clouds of ours,
In silence, her lady the bride
Is kissing the three flowers

As if they were not lilies in bloom
But holy faces indeed —
What do you carry, my lord, in the bouquet with
                                    three flowers
That brought back to life the bride's body now freed?

Translated by Dan Duțescu

MY SISTER, THE EMPRESS
[*Sora mea, împărăteasa*]

My sister, the empress
became cross with us
she took her crowns and went away
but mother and father believe
that she'll come back some day.

She is sure to come back, says father
why, how could anyone
from one kingdom to another go
with only her slippers on.

But mother has a woman's heart
she says it wouldn't be right
for her daughter to wear a crown and slippers
out in broad daylight.

She'll come tonight, says mother
she'll come tomorrow, says father
I alone know that my sister is gone
forever.

I have seen the place where she has passed
strewn with the seven crowns
so her parents wouldn't be aware
and I tracked down her slippers
in that other kingdom there.

Translated by Dan Duțescu

FORTEPIANO
[*Fortepiano*]

The portrait above the piano
Had penetrated the black, glossy wood
But the pianist was aware of nothing from his side
He would stick his fingers into his eyes
And everybody was petrified.

I myself had forgotten about everything
But while the music was elating me
Above the orchestra I discerned, I guess,
How the portrait that had fallen into the piano
Still hung motionless

Like Damocles' sword
Over the one who was playing
And he might as well see
How he was sticking his fingers into his eyes
Just as a treat to me.

A good thing he didn't know
That he was in the black, glossy wood too
And in that *salon* so terribly *triste*
Suddenly I felt that he might
Stick out his tongue at the pianist.

Translated by Dan Duțescu

NIGHTMARE
[*Coşmar*]

You had gotten completely lost between two roads
Between two directions, between two passions
Among a thousand smiling faces
During the short break between two sessions.

They were looking for you in alarm and could not find you
They said that apparantly you had something to say
Just when everybody knew
That you had gone away

For good and that you could never come back
I alone would wait deamily
For you to appear as you were when I first met you
And to tell me at last what your ailment might be.

And then you actually appeared as you once were
I could well see your face alight as I had missed it
Only your spirit I could no longer see
As if it had never existed.

Translated by Dan Duțescu

CONSTANȚA BUZEA
(1941-   )

Born in Bucharest on 31 March 1941, Constanța Buzea studied Romanian language and literature at the University of Bucharest, also working as poetry editor on various youth and student publications.

Her poetic debut was at the age of sixteen in the journal *Tînărul scriitor*, while she published her first volume, *De pe pămînt*, six years later, in 1963. Her best known poems are to be found in the volumes *Norii* (1968), *Agonice* (1970), *Coline* (1970), *Râsad de spini* (1973), *Leac pentru îngeri* (1974), and *Ape cu plute. Poezii de dragoste* (1975). In 1986, Editura Eminescu in Bucharest issued a volume of 80 Buzea poems translated into English by Sergiu Celac, *Tip of the Iceberg*.

In Buzea's poems one finds much unrest, existential meditation and — more recently — maturity and an Apollinian attitude together with tender femininity and a nostalgia for classicism.

Andrei Bantaș

DANGER
[*Pericol*]

I am both horrified and hurt
By muteness (even swans take pride
In that); it's always afloat.
I only feel myself whole at night;
It is through its mysterious voice
That can take place its murky light
My halt without lights or joys.
Writhing awfully and as if lying down
I hear the sleep in which I bleed;
I conjure some soul from the ground:
Your progress, angel, it will impede.

Translated by Andrei Bantaş

IN THE SHADOW OF THE SAME BOOK
[Umbriţi de-aceiaşi carte]

let the air circulate as in a mill
let dead leaves bury my autumn with you
let us have before us many hills
let me be ill without feeling pain

may dew fall in swarms over steppes
let the fragrance of grass evoke thirst
let young colts gather in herds
stopping the wagons drawn by mares

let us side with the same griefs and sorrows
let the sweet death of the world not take pity
on my broken soul torn by two destinies

let us resist in the shadow of the same book
when not to be and to be forever remote
are meant to bear the same image.

Translated by Andrei Bantaş

THE PREY SEES YOU
[*Prada te vede*]

angels do not have
either sex or fame

and desperate is the man who does not have
with whom to share silence

but do not hurry
the prey sees you and awaits

it is only when it runs
that you must make longer strides than it.

Translated by Andrei Bantaş

POETRY TOO IS A KIND OF SLEEP
[*Şi poezia e un somn*]

poetry too is a kind of sleep
out of which you never wake

with your eyes wide open under the seas
dreaming of wordly spasms

crying you set pearls on your eyelids
and you whiten your lips with salt

an unfortunate stranger estranged
among pirate's treasures

regrets at not understanding
the movement of fish mouths

in the quiet of monsters being devoured
at least of them you must beware

without being entirely received
you are neither drowned nor alive

to be able to slam a heavy gate
to draw the curtains over windows

poetry too is a kind of sleep
out of which you never wake

Translated by Andrei Bantaş

WAITING FOR HAMLET
[*Aşteptîndu-l pe Hamlet*]

alone
paining the marble womb
always everywhere is born
revelation

you hit like a defeated man

I am listening in the light
to the crash of window panes
words mingled with tears
that have not yet come forth

you are in vain waiting to be greeted
by hamlet.

Translated by Andrei Bantaş

ANA BLANDIANA
(1942-   )

The poet Ana Blandiana is one of the most widely known figures in Romania today. Her stature in the public life of her country derives from two sources: first, from her reputation for, and long history of, dissidence and resistance as a writer, and second, from her prominent role during and after the December 1989 revolution which overthrew the Ceauşescu dictatorship under which she had been banned a number of times. In January 1990 she was briefly a member of the Council of the provisional National Salvation Front government, from which she resigned in protest after only three weeks. More recently, since July, 1991, she has served as President of the Civic Alliance, a coalition of non-partisan opposition interests which she helped found in November 1990. But if a spokesperson for independent-mindedness in her country, to which in her writings she expresses a loyal attachment, she is also rightly celebrated as one of its strongest poetic voices of the late twentieth century and one of the most important and representative contemporary figures in Romanian literary tradition; and this high esteem for her poetic accomplishment is becoming worldwide.

Ana Blandiana (whose given name is Otilia-Valeria Coman) was born on 25 March 1942 in Timişoara, the cosmopolitan western Romanian city that was once part of the Austro-Hungarian Empire and where, in fact, the December 1989 revolt began. She went to secondary school in the city of Oradea, farther north near the border with Hungary, and in 1967 graduated from the University of Cluj-Napoca in Romania's Transylvanian region. She then moved to Bucharest, where she worked as an editor of *Amfiteatru*, the student literary magazine, and as a librarian in the Institute of Fine Arts, though she would soon give her full attention to writing, not only poetry but also stories, children's works, and journalistic columns of literary and social comment.

Blandiana began to publish poetry in 1959 at the age of seventeen, when she first signed her work with her chosen pen name, and her initial volume, *Persoane întîia plural*, appeared in 1964. Since then, she has written many important books and collections of poetry, and her volumes of poetry now total over a dozen, with an additional nine books of prose and further works for children.

Blandiana's poems have also appeared in over twenty-five countries, and in 1990 a selection from her poetry, entitled *The Hour of Sand*, was issued in England, translated by Peter Jay and Anca Cristofovici. The poet has won many prizes for her writing, and from 1974 through the summer of 1988, a column under her signature was a regular and much-read feature of the major literary weekly, *România literară*, with some interruptions during times she was officially declared unpublishable.

The cessation of Blandiana's column a year and a half before the fall of the Ceauşescu government coincided with the third time that her writings and her name were banned from Romanian periodicals, publishing houses, and media. The first occasion happened after her debut in print when, despite her using a pseudonym, all the country's reviews received a communication that the author (whose father was a persecuted priest) was the daughter of an enemy of the people in prison. This ban lasted four years until what in fact became another debut in 1963. The second period in which her work was forbidden lasted for only three months in 1985 because of West European protests. It followed the publication of four protest poems she had sent to the student review she once worked on, *Amfiteatru*, but did not expect to see printed. Three years later, in August 1988, Blandiana was silenced again, with a book of new poems halted and no publication of any kind permitted except for a collection of largely previously printed work, *Poezii*, her fourth anthology of selected works, which was released only after a strong letter of protest she wrote in March, 1989, to President Ceauşescu.

The recent detour of Ana Blandiana's career into public spheres is all the more remarkable given the character of her literary voice, for which even her journalistic essays were (in an ongoing Romanian prose convention) metaphorical and contemplative occasions in the development and expression of sensibility and the inner self. Blandiana's lyricism reflects both a highly traditional poetics and a highly individualistic persona at the same time. It is fitting that her debut opened the brief interlude of relatively free speech between the post-war Stalinism (and literary proletarian realism) of the Soviet occupation period and the Ceauşescu regime's totalitarian control that steadily intensified for twenty years through the 1970s and on until the end of 1989.

With a tone that is personal, even intimate at times, but never confessional, her poems celebrate the imagination and conceive of a kind of inward salvation, employing vivid imagery, often drawn from the natural world, and a melodious and evocative language. The poet expresses her complex vision with a poetic purity that is one the greatest satisfactions of a Blandiana poem, infusing her works with a serene and reflexive spirit and quiet joy that even her bleakest themes cannot efface. Thus in a sense it may be among the least surprising contradictions of contemporary Romanian culture that this essentially apolitical, rather traditionally Romantic poet of beauty and individual revelation found strength in an intrinsic privacy but at the same time, in a corresponding independence of spirit, found authority to speak out for the common good.

Adam J. Sorkin

THE GIFT
[*Darul*]

My gift is tragic, like some ancient punishment.
What ancestor of mine so sinned that I'm condemned to
                                wear laurels of guilt?
All I touch turns into words
As in the legend of King Midas.

I feel close to him, the king who died from the curse
Of his hand's turning everything into gold.
He died starving, unable to eat the bread
Desiccated into gold, unable to nibble at the water.

I cannot look at the sky — it clouds over with words.
Can I bite into apple enclosed in the names of colors?
Love, if I touch it, patterns itself into sentences.
Oh woe unto me, woe unto the one punished with praises.

Woe unto me, oh woe, the trees do not shed leaves,
It's only words that each autumn drop yellow and old.
I love high mountains, but the mountains tremble
Under the burden of copulating syllables.

I wish I could gather all the words in one place
And set them on fire, to undress the world of them,
But then the world's skin would become rough and coarse,
Like the handsome prince with a pig's skin in the fairy tale

At once with them would also burn the world
Stuck to the inner surface of words, as in an album...
Is it that I don't know how to detach them, or is it now
                                   impossible for me
To detach the world from my world of words?

Translated by Adam J. Sorkin and Ioana Ieronim

PURITY, I KNOW
[*Ştiu puritatea*]

Purity, I know, cannot bear fruit,
Virgins cannot have progeny.
Such is the great principle of stain,
Paid tribute in order to be.

Blue butterflies grow caterpillars,
The flowers grow into ripe fruit.
Only snow is immaculate white,
The warm earth is impure at the root.

Unsoiled eternity sleeps and sleeps,
In the air microbes dance all around.
You may, should you choose, avoid being born,
If you are, you'll end down in the ground.

In your thought, the word stays happy,
Once said, the ear slanders its aim.
Toward which side of the scale shall I bend —
Voiceless dream or resounding fame?

Between silence and sin, which shall I choose —
Between herds and the lotus vying?
Oh, the drama of dying all in white
Or conquering but nonetheless dying...

Translated by Adam J. Sorkin and Ioana Ieronim

WE SHOULD
[*Ar trebui*]

We should be born old,
Should arrive in the world wise,
Be able to determine our destiny on earth,
Understand at the initial crossroads what ways to set out
on
And know irresponsibility only in our longing to go forth.
Then we should grow younger, ever younger, in our going,
Mature and forceful in order to reach the gate of creation,
Should pass through it to enter love as teenagers,
Become children at the birth of our children.
Then they would be older than we,
They would teach us to talk, would rock us to sleep,
We would vanish more and more, become smaller and ever
smaller,
Like a grape from a bunch, a pea from a pod, a grain from
a sheaf of wheat...

Translated by Adam J. Sorkin

BITTER BODY
[Trup amar]

Scent of a body abandoned by its soul
Under the shameless sun,
Scent of a body on which
The flesh keeps growing,
In which the blood is bubbling,
And, in a kind of frentic squall,
Each cell couples with another...
Don't come near me, don't touch me,
My body is poisonous and bitter,
With sun oozing from my armpits,
And butterflies besotted with me incited
Out of the fractured larvae of desires
They can no more comprise. Flee, flee!
From the arms of the defiling cross
On which, happy, it's myself I despise.
Don't breathe in the intoxicating smell,
When the soul forsakes me as the sun is high
So I may capture you, and you crucify.

Translated by Adam J. Sorkin and Ioana Ieronim

STAR BLOWN IN THE WIND
[*Stea adusă de vînt*]

From the first you were blown in the wind
Like a seed.
I quipped: "No one's ever wished on
A star blown in the wind."
But afterwards,
When you fixed yourself on my forehead
And began sprouting,
I understood that you *are* a seed.
Insatiable, savagely piercing into my brain
With relentless rays conceiving roots,
You are a seed.
It's such a pity
That the plant you germinate,
Light from light,
Can become visible
Only after
I have set into darkness.

Translated by Adam J. Sorkin

ARCHITECTURE IN MOVEMENT
[*Arhitectură-n mişcare*]

Who or what could ever make it cease,
This moving, changing architecture
Forever born, forever dying,
This monastery which approaches me
Nearing, swelling, growing, and here it is,
With arching vaults and domes of spray
Like nightcaps of foam and crowns suspending,
Rushing upwards in the air, dissipating itself slowly,
                                then downwards tossing,
Breaking itself into a cloud of jellyfish, of algae, of crabs
And streaming within the ground?

Who could ever arrest in stone-like stasis
This riot of movement too alive not to die
And too mortal not to be reborn?
Who could call out to the waves, "Be still!"

And bid the waters fail to be a sea,
And this ever crumbling monastery
Collapsing into itself like echo's last decibel
Have hatch its columns changed to bone
In the air walling round it like a shell?

Translated by Adam J. Sorkin and Maria-Ana Tupan

CALCIUM MOLECULES
[*Molecule de calciu*]

I'm in no hurry,
I'll let time pass by,
Each second as it drops
Bit by bit erodes
Suffering.
I'll be patient.
Each wave that breaks
Is rasp to the rock
On which I'm bound,
Each speck of rust
Thins the chain.
In just a millennium, or two,
The rock will become sand,
The iron links fine powder,
My bones calcium molecules
Dissolved in water,
Suffering nothing.

Translated by Adam J. Sorkin

A STRAIGHT LINE
[O linie dreaptă]

A straight line, like so,
A bold line
Between the two halves of the page.
Thus the possibility of insisting:
On one side or on the other.
But alas, the paper sucks it in,
And the line is replaced by a colony
Of worms crawling
From one side to the other
Through the earth furrowed by the pen.
Wriggling and wavering,
Yet advancing, advancing,
Devouring the boundary and the ink.
The moral of this song:
Ask not the executioner
To distinguish right and wrong.

Translated by Adam J. Sorkin and Maria-Ana Tupan

OBSESSION
[*Obsesie*]

Would I love you, I wonder, as much as I do
Were you fearsome and mighty
Like others? Would I think so much
Of you were you triumphant
And savage at war?
Would I have dreamt of you
In such anxiety were you master
Of others? Just as the children
Of fortunate families can leave home
When they are grown, free of any responsibility,
And go off, if they feel like it, remembering
No one there, while all the time
The children of the poor have to return
To assist their families, sending
Packages and money, supporting the younger ones
In school, so in the same way the fortunate
Poets of bigger peoples
Can forget about their source, they can depart,
They can be in world's...
Would you also be my obsession, I wonder, were you
Fortunate? Had you been able to
Oppress, to subjugate, to spread enmity?
O Goddess of History, unbind from curse and set free
Our future with immeasurable generosity!

Translated by Adam J. Sorkin and Ioana Ieronim

BALLAD
[*Baladă*]

I have no other Ana:
Myself I build into the wall.
Yet who can say this will do the trick
When the wall does not crumble
All on its own
But is rammed down by the mad caprice
Of a somnambulist bulldozer
Careering helter-skelter through a nightmare.
So once again I build,
It's as though I've built a wave,
A second day once more,
And a third time,
A fourth time,
This monastery liquid to the last clock's tick
Foredoomed to fling to ruin on the shore;
Yet once again I build, now lime,
Now brick,
And without a flaw
A creature
For the crossbeam
Of the haunted dream:
Ana has no other Ana
And less and less often
Even her own self
Has Ana.

Translated by Adam J. Sorkin

GRETE TARTLER
(1948-   )

Grete Tartler was born in Bucharest on 28 November 1948. She studied the viola at the "Ciprian Porumbescu" Conservatory, and later majored in Arabic and English at the University of Bucharest.

After graduating, she taught the viola for fifteen years before becoming editor of *Neue Literatur*, a famous literary magazine in Romania, edited in German. Her work with German and Romanian culture led to her recent appointment as cultural attaché at the Romanian Embassy in Vienna. She is also presently working toward a Ph.D. in the history of philosophy.

Tartler is a prolific writer. Thus far she has published seven books of poetry, four of nursery rhymes for children, two books of essays, an anthology of contemporary German poetry, as well as numerous translations of German and Arabic literature and poetry in Romanian. In 1989 Oxford University Press published a collection of her poems, entitled *Orient Express*, translated into English by the British poet Fleur Adcock. She received a prize from the British Poetry Society for this volume. Her poetry has also been appreciated in her native country, receiving prizes from the Romanian Writers' Union in 1978 and 1985, as well as the prize of the Romanian Academy in 1982.

Liviu Bleoca

CONCERTO FOR UNICORN AND TAPE (I)
[*Concert pentru licorn şi bandă magnetică (I)*]

You step onto the stage,
while, talented and pure,
with the confidence of one who's recorded his own voice
earlier, in the studio;
the voice of someone yet unborn, a voice that you'll carry
all throughout your life;
"The tape is rolling! Play-back!"
                            and your lips

synchronize with the heavenly tape —
this blank tape recording is the only thing
you understood correctly:
you speak of things you've never seen,
you sing a love aria with falsettos in the higher registers,
and look how praiseworthy you are for the art of
self-mimicking!
Scorpions swarm under the floor, you trample on them,
the curtain moves from the deepness of your breath,
a young woman in the stalls
starts crying,
you wait impatiently
for the well-deserved bouquet of poison hemlock.

But a day comes when the tape breaks.

Let me see you *now*:
you can only cry out
the truth with *your own* voice,
otherwise you'll be devoured by the eyes of those awaiting
you can only
cry out the truth with your own voice.

Translated by Liviu Bleoca

WHY DO YOU CARE FOR EMINESCU'S WOMAN?
[*Ce-ţi pasă de iubita lui Eminescu*]

A poet calls me up and says:
it is high time
we did something — Eminescu
and Veronica
should be buried together.

In the archaeology review, the skeleton
of a superb Neandrathal man —
I wonder where his woman lies,
why weren't they buried together.

Nor is Novalis beside his beloved Sophie.
What times, oh, what times we live in, when
poets are still worrying
over the lover's fate after death!

Maybe we'll be luckier, if we stay in good health.

Translated by Liviu Bleoca

THE MAKING OF THE POEM
[*Facerea poemului*]

One May day
and I rush into the poppy field
as if I conjure initiation:
twisted smoke,
a whirlwind
amidst the weeds, and only
later my arms rising like written
pages — writing materials on the fly.
You laugh and say to me:
Keep your eyes closed,
and neither drink nor eat for three days, then
prepare large salverfuls of dainties —
if you can leave them aside
for this wild smoke, then,
yes, you are allowed to try.

Translated by Liviu Bleoca

MEDIEVAL ROMANCE
[*Roman medieval*]

For years I have studied the secret
of Gothic courtyards shining after the rain.
A bucketful of water:
when I shake it,
the old woman at the window is my daughter,
she watches me with large eyes, without a smile,
having no mouth or anything to be really *hers*.

> You remember the Saxon porcelain master
> who had disclosed the secrets of kaolin to his daughter,
> out of love,
> and she disclosed them out of love to a young man,
> then she threw herself into the hot kiln...

For years I have learned how to kill dragons,
but I have never met dragons, nobody needs
such an art. Still, I haven't disclosed
its secret.
Now I'm pulling out the weeds,
the large, vigorous leaves that sway
when I lie down among them.
We all have equally ringed eyes.

In the nearby oak tree
a nightingale started singing.

Translated by Liviu Bleoca

SAHEL
[*Sahel*]

Every year the desert
      (with *d* from *devils*)
advances fifteen kilometers
      (with *k* from *karma*)
dries up springs
      (with *s* from *spirits*)
dries up more and more words.
The dictionary is ever more famished —
essences on the leap
stop for a second over the abyss,
then whiten the cracked earth.
The poet watches
the pure skulls of the words;
the words, still living and hungry,
watch the poet.

Translated by Liviu Bleoca

AT THE BASIS OF GREAT ROADS
[*La temelia marilor drumuri*]

At the basis of great bridges,
at the basis of great roads,
there is, from their construction
a small opening
meant to simplify, at some time or another
their being blown up.
Oh, the built-in death watch accepted
under the walls of great buildings,
this terrible help.
And our bodies scouring
the great roads on white bicycles,
haven't they carried from birth
cells for the sudden
— still unknown —
explosive?

Translated by Liviu Bleoca

A SUFI LEGEND
[*O legendă sufi*]

A strange story:
it goes that a Sufi reached the land of the fools
who were afraid of a melon
thinking it was a green dragon.
That Sufi cut the melon
but in his turn was cut by the fools,
who were even more deeply afraid
of a dragon slayer.
I would have won their confidence
and would have accepted it was a monster —
in fact that's what I did,
I gradually showed them what a melon is,
I taught them how to grow it,
Then its creeping stem covered my window
a yellow fruit grows bigger and bigger, it swells,
it darkens my room —
though I'm not good at it, I'll have to cut
its stem and its yellow brain
which is grinning in the sky —
I should put down the stem and the monster.
I'd have more light
to find this poem
an optimistic ending.

Translated by Rodica Albu

DANIELA CRĂSNARU
(1950-   )

Daniela Crăsnaru, poet, fiction writer, author of children's books, and editor, was born on 14 April 1950 in Craiova, an ancient regional capital and, in modern times, small industrial city on the Wallachian plain between the Carpathian mountains and the Danube. She attended the University of Craiova, from which she graduated with a degree in Romanian and English in 1973. The same year as her graduation also saw the publication of Crăsnaru's first volume of poetry, *Lumina cît umbra*, by the prominent Romanian publishing house, Editura Eminescu, for which the poet worked as an editor until two years before the revolution.

Crăsnaru's works now number over a dozen including two volumes of short stories and three books of poetry for children. The poet has won three major awards: Romanian Writer's Union poetry prizes for 1979 and 1982 and the Award of the Romanian Academy for 1988, which, despite the date, was awarded after the December 1989 overthrow of the Ceauşescus. This last recognition, given for career achievement, was the first Academy prize following the freeing of the decision-making process from the political pressures and Communist Party cronyism that had emptied the award of literary significance by the mid-1980's. In 1991, the Oxford Poets Series published an anthology of her works, *Letters from Darkness*, translated by Fleur Adcock. The book includes "drawer poems" from a notebook of works Crăsnaru would not publish before the change of government.

Daniela Crăsnaru's themes and subjects show an important evolution throughout her career, an evolution that places her, with Blandiana, at the forefront of a remarkable group of postwar Romanian women poets. Early in her career, Crăsnaru's poems were lyrical and emotionally refined, a deeply affecting sensual evocation of fleeting emotions in a kind of exalted psychological state of poetic grace and subdued personal confessiveness, but her works became more sarcastic, more skeptical in tone, more disillusioned. Her writing from the 80's on remains intensely imagistic but is also intensely ironic; her lines are thus powerful in feeling and highly concentrated, often both melancholy and a touch grotesque, at once stoic, despairing, and transcendent. The demanding tension and complexity of Crăsnaru's poetics created both a thematic and emotional center in a mood of stagnation, entrapment, and suffocation and, as well, a self-conscious thickness of texture that was a device to elude state censorship by an intentional over-determination of the text. At the same time, her works evidence an explicit concern with writing that orients her later work somewhat towards the direction of more recent post-modernist poetic practices.

Since the revolution, Crăsnaru has gone back to editorial work, in the spring of 1990 becoming director of Romania's leading publisher of children's literature, the Ion Creangă Publishing House, which is now in the process of privatization. Also in the spring of 1990, along with other writers and intellectuals, she ran for parliament in the new government. She campaigned as a non-party member on the National Salvation Front (FSN) candidate lists and was elected, serving for two years as a deputy. In the 1992 elections, Crăsnaru chose not to run again, although she remains active in politics.

Adam J. Sorkin

THE REHEARSAL STAGE
[*Sala de repetiţii*]

The rehearsal stage. The coolness, the half-light.
We are resuming. Refining our action.
The very same action.
Its obscure corpse
abandoned under a swarm of devouring words.
The director calls out, Run through it once again.
Take it from there, from hatred. No, from there,
                              from tenderness,
from there, from hesitation.
Reach within, hold on, breathe deep!
Come close to the chalk mark
to the center, to the core
from which only the true gestures can spring, will
                              spring forth
the genuine attitudes for which we have
so great a need.
Sure, sure, you have the right to choose between a
                              pirouette
and a curtsy, between going on your knees
and crawling, between collapse and flight.
Just be more natural!
For Christ's sake, try to imagine
that over there's the water, and further on, the skirt
                              of the forest
that only a little more is left, about three speeches,
and a saving hand will haul you up by the hair,
will eventually pluck you out
of that whirlpool swirling ceaselessly.
Close your eyes. That's it...

Imagine that the wind is blowing softly, so softly,
that you're home, that you're ten,
that your mother and your father are alive
so very youthful and so very happy
and only now are you to make that central speech
which sustains the entire scaffolding,
this entire classical action of this classical text
which we haven't any means of changing
not through lighting, not through scenery, not
                              through direction.
There's no choice here after all. Is this clear to you?
If so, then let's resume.
From despair. No. From confusion. No, no.
From the beginning.

Translated by Adam J. Sorkin and Maria-Ana Tupan

[UNTITLED]

As evening fell, with you my poem has also dawdled
and with you the emperor's fabled steed
fattened on embers, with you moon, with you
misfortune, with you silver scorpion. With all of you
my words have gone, holy servant maids,
you whose feet I bathed
(all in my mind).
Now I await the annunciation, the augury
the golden child in the golden manger on that pale pale day
which is going to swallow me.

Translated by Adam J. Sorkin and Ioana Ieronim

THE WINDOW IN THE WALL
[Fereastra în zid]

Along the wall and flush up against it
with hands stretched wide with face glued to it
breath returning into the nostrils
infused with moist darkness
one step one day another step another day
here is where it should be
exactly here the window really *is*
the rectangle of gray.

With chalk-covered hands I caress its frame
as if I caressed your shoulders your thighs
what operatic light might pour in from outside
what an uproar of scorching saps.
And what else might I devise in your absence:
a downpour in mocking torrents an English park
through which bound with enormous leaps
the hunting hounds
the sky gray flagstone
supported by my own breathing
a hill in the background
ignoring all the rules of classical perspective
a golgotha of lead overgrown
with interjections, moaned and diminutive.
And what else might lie outside this window
which I don't have the courage to break through
though I cannot open it at all
this window sketched clumsily
chalked roughly there by me
on the wall.

Translated by Adam J. Sorkin and Maria-Ana Tupan

WRITING LESSON
[Lecţia de scris]

I'll have to repeat the course.
The professor says:
Describe that waterfall
dazzling and majestic
in the sunrise.
I stand with eyes staring
at an anemic thread of water
trickling into the mouth of a drain
and I say in all humility, I can't
no, I can't.
You lack wings, the professor says
you lack the tiniest scrap of metaphysics.
Repeat after me now:
whiteness dazzle brilliance crystal
(ecstasy).
Whiteness dazzle perfumed words
in lace so neatly starched
through which with great impertinence
reality feverishly gushes
like blood through an antiseptic
bandage.
My concluding argument:
last summer on the beach
the last word of a drowned man
dragged upon the shore
was the very stream of water
rushing out from his lungs.

I saw it with my own eyes: no
immaculate petals no
wings of butterflies.
Blood and water seeping into sand.

You fail the exam and you'll have to repeat
the professor says and he pushes me into the emptiness
of the seventh floor of the school.
He pretends not to see.
I pretend not to die.

Translated by Adam J. Sorkin and Maria-Ana Tupan

HARP OF BLOOD
[*Harfa de sînge*]

How unnatural and pale this hand writing
it touches the things I once loved
fragments of time

your torso
on which my shadow draws hieroglyphics
obsessively.

Let's read them, let's read them
my blood cries out delirious
let's know what's there
let's explore that far
to the ultimate consequences so to speak

but two of us —
this hand that writes and the written letter it made —
oh, how afraid we are.

Translated by Adam J. Sorkin and Sergiu Celac

LOST POEM
[*Poemul pierdut*]

"Look what they've done to my song!" You, they, all of you,
each one any way he could.
Take a sheet of paper and write. Reconstruct the poem.
At the Linnaeus Museum they reconstructed an animal from
                                                                a phalange
and now rows of bored pupils stare at it.

There are animals and animals.
This wild beast will kill me.
This one is cast from a mold. This one gets stuffed
                                                        with cotton.
This one doesn't exist.
She has ferocious maxillaries, she has syllables.
She will kill me. He.
This lost poem torn into pieces
inside a ridiculous taxi.
"Look what they've done to my song!" Every last thing
they could.

Like a soldier at Marathon my soul reaches the month
                                                        of December.

I forgot, it says, striking against the clenched teeth.
This is a sentence of victory.
Meanwhile I'm trying to reconstruct a poem
which I can no longer remember any part of.

I did it.

Translated by Adam J. Sorkin and Mia Nazarie

DEFINITION OF LOSS
[*O definiție a pierderii*]

A definition of loss by absorption.
The sea swallows the shore
and its wave is of stone
and of earth.
My brain
much more than my body embraces you
and you are of syllable and of word.
Only my eye still lies in wait for you
its ray follows your scent, invents you
refashions you for the thousandth time
my blind eye that does not see
that does not see anything
outwardly.

Translated by Adam J. Sorkin and Mia Nazarie

THE HEMISPHERES OF MAGDEBURG
[*Emisferele de Magdeburg*]

My flesh is getting bored
your fingers are already tired.
Soon we shall see the dentures, the teflon parts,
the machinery of this supernatural state
soon we shall be able to conjugate again, without trembling
I am, you are
separate, separate
our intact cells
will forget absolutely every clause
our confused instincts will lay down
their muzzle
upon their dazed paws.
No, it's not the explosion stalking the ventricle that
                                                    worries me
not the scarlet blaze of this state of mind
not the adrenalin shock that I fear
not this small flame here
ever smaller
but this love, hopelessly twinned
nearly incestuous
between our two occiputs thinking
the same word both at once.

Translated by Adam J. Sorkin and Sergiu Celac

HERESY
[*Erezie*]

Really, I once had
such great potential

Really, I diagrammed for him
the Bermuda triangle
on just a few torrid inches.
Hey, you soul in a dog collar! Hey, flesh with ridges!
Hey, you dizzy blood bloated with birdshot!
He was prepared for soft drugs
for pygmy illusions. Not
for an extraterrestrial lady — he'd never seen one;
for him
nobody had ever landed from the skies.

Really, rotting away at the tip of his collar
I was his cyanide like a spy's.

Translated by Adam J. Sorkin and Sergiu Celac

THE MONSTER
[*Monstrul*]

I don't have a memory. I've labored hard
for that.
I've used my claws and teeth to dig out
every instant gone by
from the carcass still pulsing with blood.
I've nothing that ever happened.
All the happenings that were mine
belong to others now.
I out-live. I'm looking behind me
and my look engenders where I've gone
pillars of salt and mountains of tears
turned to stone.

Translated by Adam J. Sorkin and Ioana Ieronim

ELENA ȘTEFOI
(1954-   )

Born in Boroaia in the county of Suceava in northern
Moldavia on 19 July 1954, Elena Ștefoi made her poetical debut
in the literary journal *Amfiteatru* in 1975. In 1980 she graduated
from the University of Bucharest with a degree in Philology. Her
first book of poems, *Linia de plutire*, won the prize of the
Romanian Academy for best debut volume in 1983.

In addition to her poetry, Ștefoi has published short stories and
essays and has worked as an editor on various literary publications.
Presently, she is an editor at *Dilema*, one of the leading cultural
journals in post-communist Romania, published under the auspicies
of the Romanian Cultural Foundation.

Rodica Albu

THROUGH YOUNG BLOOD VESSELS
[*Prin tinere vase de singe*]

Backward and forward:
a hostile pile of gold.
Slowly, little by little,
it destroys
the classical organ of speech.
(Oh, that wailing darkening
hills and valleys, a worm
between reason and passion,
my love
my love mounted up
that the whole district can see it!)
Through young blood vessels
somberly filled
shrieks the daily beast.
And, when you are absent, she gives me for nothing
the necessary helping of air
sayings and proverbs,
the marvel.

Translated by Rodica Albu

MUCH LATER
[*Mult mai tîrziu*]

I used to mercilessly slap
the mouth of the volcano.

Now I hardly dare breathe
under the golden boots
of the tale.

About all this
much later
someone will talk
and someone else
will tell him he's lying.

Translated by Rodica Albu

ODE TO ALMIGHTY REMEMBRANCE
[*Oda atotputernicei amintiri*]

Crumpled darknesses, cackling,
wait for the Last Supper.
I'm longing for
the purely theoretical
restlessness
I'm longing for
seasickness
for the wild whirlwind
in the sole
of the rope dancer.
I look back:
the same girl
— an old hag from the day
she threw the first clods
into the family grave —
is still trying to persuade
the same camel caravan
to go through the needle's eye.

Translated by Rodica Albu

ODE TO WISE SILENCES
[Oda tacerilor inţelepte]

Mother's last smile
tattered pervades
the tin gate
of the air.
Like a swarm
of joyful wasps
rises the cold in the womb
like a swarm of wasps
the remains of the diadem
attack the sight.
How can I help
the shadow of my own disappearance
harnessed
to the plow day and night?

Translated by Rodica Albu

A SKETCH FROM NATURE
[Schiţa după natura]

Under the summer sky
arabesques and parentheses,
claps
between the vocal cords
and the sound,
the group of minor characters
in love, playing
with fire balls.
This still nature
stays still.
I furtively fumbled
in a chest.
Now I unlock it with keys that fit:
in it there's a blizzard raging
to the other end
of the world.

Translated by Rodica Albu

MARTA PETREU
(1955-   )

Marta Petreu was born on 14 March 1955 in Jucu near Cluj-Napoca where she later attended the University, graduating with a degree in philosophy in 1980. After finishing her studies she spent several years teaching high school before becoming an editor of *România literară* in Bucharest and *Steaua* in Cluj, two of the most important literary magazines in Romania.

Following the overthrow of the communist regime in December, 1989, she founded and became editor-in-chief of a new monthly literary journal, *Apostrof*, in Cluj-Napoca. The editors of this magazine are all writers and critics of the younger generation of intellectuals in Romania. At the national book fair held in Cluj in 1991, *Apostrof* shared the prize for the best cultural magazine of the year.

Thus far, Petreu has published three volumes of poems, her first winning a prize from the Romanian Writers' Union for best debut volume in 1981, and a book of essays. In addition to her literary activities, she has also completed a Ph.D. in philosophy. Some of her poems have also been translated into English and published in a volume that appeared in England. The poems presented here are from Petreu's latest book, *Loc psihic*.

Liviu Bleoca

PSYCHIC PLACE I
[*Loc psihic I*]

Pains — minatures of hell

Who assures me night after night
that in a foreseeable future everything will be all right
who speaks to me

I'm here. I'm a stranger

Whole books have been written on the impure crises
                                        of melancholy
enough lies have been said
But for your benefit
I can still imagine delicate landscapes
in just a few words I can counterfeit reality:
as I stand on winter dusk — infants
of hebephrenia — on an iceberg

Today I say about suffering: reality overwhelms imagination
the same way the wards of an ordinary hospital
humiliate Hell

Who assures me
that in a foreseeable future everything will be all right
who speaks to me
whom should I call in the night
when in the miraculous transparency of ideas
I can't protect my brain my eyes
just with my bare hands?

Translated by Liviu Bleoca

SUNDAY AUCTION
[*Licitație de duminică*]

We keep on bidding for miscarried projects:
engagement and childhood — I declare
birth against nature — I cry out
a still young venomous woman — I think

And you: young mortal and venomous:
cast off appearances and hopes like a nun's
habit
rewrite into a new tongue all sacred books (the lost ones)
relearn metaphysics (a patched up and sensual one)
invent an ultimate word like anguish
build up an innocent religion for all the slums of the world

So: young mortal and venomous:
out of my skull as from a clandestine brothel
long rows of women walk away into the night;
I am secluded inside my memory as in a maternity ward
Therefore memory. Mole! — I insult it. Plump mole.
Blind. Velvety like wickedness: you nibble at the roots
                                          of the grass
and at the nerves under the skin. You gorged one!
                              save whatever you can
that is the leftovers the rag fair that is nothingness

We bid for miscarried projects:
engagement and childhood — I declare
birth against nature — I cry out
brain without pain centers — I whimper

Translated by Liviu Bleoca

RED SHIFT
[*Fuga spre roşu*]

Writers die. Poets die. Ah.

Ah. Now they are cannon fodder
in the mute war that is being fought
Look at their illuminating hair

We know: they are people like everybody
They step out of rank by writing. They carry
their uncorrupted brain their mortal brain on their shoulders
I know: their brain
like the brain of my father Augustine
yes — it rots
like a library on fire
their body disintegrates in the earth

And they keep coming. And they keep dying. They are
                                        cannon fodder
they still write they describe
how the earth grows old:
the same way galaxies fade away with a red shift
Under the earth on the earth libraries burn their nerves burn
shuddering

And they keep coming. And they keep dying.

Translated by Liviu Bleoca

PSYCHIC PLACE II
[*Loc psihic II*]

I'm here. These texts these sacred carnivorous words
this verbal membrane
(read carefully I summon you read twice!):
curtain meninx electroshock therapy
blanket straitjacket
bed-sheet hymen placenta

I praise this osmotic verbal membrane
I give you I get undressed I curse myself
Ah! my repressed whorish pathos:
I give you lucidly
Any poetic art is written in ink
(I calmly assure in public)
in fact
in these mortal neurons

Darkness and dust

These texts these words I've picked from books and streets
Only this ultimate membrane
(ah! precious like the hymen
fragile like soap bubbles)
still separates me
from the psychic place where you've pushed me
                    as toward the springs of the Nile
from the psychic place whence I try — cautiously

painfully — to pull out:
my hands my paws my brain my heart
What is beyond? darkness and dust
What is left? a poetic art this darkness this dust
these cracking neurons

Translated by Liviu Bleoca

THE BABYLONIAN LOTTERY
[*Loteria din Babilonia*]

This is my Sunday dress
my approximately untouched body is underneath
my informal soul is at the back beyond
And this is you
hopelessly in love with me
that is with a simply fictitious
and completely unlocalizable reality

What is my role among these unpaired lives
that only chance has put
together
with the following commandment: be fruitful
and multiply in number like the sands on the sea
you will earn thy sleep by the sweat of thy brow
Or: love thy neighbor more
than thyself

What am I supposed to do with all these narcissist lives?

This is you casting the die
on a Sunday

Translated by Liviu Bleoca

MARIANA MARIN
(1956-   )

Mariana Marin was born on 10 February 1956 in Bucharest. Her parents separated when she was three, and the poet-to-be was brought up by her mother, a weaver in a cooperative, and by her grandmother. She was educated in Bucharest and went on to receive a degree in philology from the University of Bucharest. After graduation, she spent ten years as a grade school teacher and also worked as a librarian before concentrating on her writing.

Marin's first collection of poems, *Un război de o sută de ani*, was published in 1981, establishing her reputation as a poet as well as her prominence among the young writers who made their debut in the early 1980's. The book won the Romanian Writers' Union prize for a first volume. Marin's next volume, her 1986 *Aripa secretă*, in part based on the strategy of presenting her stark insights in the form of a kind of fantastic lyrical diary of, and dialogue with, Anne Frank, was a slender and deeply felt book. In it, the poet made of the young woman's temporary hiding out in the captivity of the secret attic of a building in Amsterdam and her martyrdom in a concentration camp in Belsen a disguised metaphor for life in contemporary Romania, a vehicle for meanings which could not be openly acknowledged before 1989. A familiar pretense among Romanian writers since World War II, Marin's employment of the coded allusion to another repressive, murderous time and place is shrewd and effective, though of course the strategy is imposed from necessities outside the poems themselves.

Marin's poems often have moments of difficulty, with demanding and seeming opaque imagery and knots of syntax; but they are powerful, even obsessive, though frequently austere in their symbolic vocabulary and aggressive in their critical perspective and the detailed immediacy of their depiction of human life as waking, everyday nightmare. As in the work of many other important women poets over the last third of this century in

Romania, Marin's poetry shows little or no tendency toward verbal wit and linguistic play, but, rather, it is solemnly expressionistic in its mood of somber, tragic resignation. Her imagination turns towards the macabre and the brutish, and most of her works are grave reflections on the denial of human integrity and morality in an ironic landscape of mocked ideals, cynicism, distrust, and mortality. Yet, like others in her self-proclaimed post-modernist generation, she is conscious of writing as a verbal construct, and her poems at times define their universe by what seems their very resistance to many of the traditional pleasure-giving virtues of their esthetic medium.

After 1990, Mariana Marin divided her time between Paris, where a dual-language French-Romanian volume of her works was put together in the late 1980's when she was unpublishable in Romania, and Bucharest, where the poet works at the independent-spirited literary-cultural journal reflecting opposition sentiment, *Contrapunct.*

Adam J. Sorkin

ELEGY I
[*Elegie I*]

You no longer know
why it's so hard to keep on living.
Just as in the Middle Ages when disturbances in the mind
were assumed to result from disturbances of the stomach
you are now looking for a cause
(a meager boil supposing itself a revolution)
in something that gnaws and gnaws deep inside
without ever managing to reach you.

Translated by Adam J. Sorkin and Mia Nazarie

THE WATER TOWER
[*Castelul de apă*]

A hundred years' war
at the crossroads of the commercial routes
— I knew well what was in store for me!
Here I am, therefore,
slowly rotating the machinery of my sickened glance
towards the corkscrewing sounds
which bring my celestial idiom to a culmination.
Shall I relate the futility of remembrance
in my ferociously youthful midst of the facts?
Or (even better) my secluded way
through the whitish smog of the elements
one winter morning?
Shall I bring fiction to a halt right here,
on the steps of the water tower
built between the two wars
castellated like a predictable recollection
and just like it in sweetness?
Or (even better) in contemporary catacombs
set the machinery of my glance moving
toward the trembling and fright of those who read me?
But the facetious eye comes and taps me on the shoulder:
"Honey, I've seen them just like you before!"

Even better this way,
nurturing the celestial seeding
around the water tower
castellated and sweet
with every sort of crime on its flags...

Translated by Adam J. Sorkin and Mia Nazarie

TRADITION
[*Tradiţie*]

A tradition binds me to you, Anne.
A tradition below sea level
just like this Dutch landscape now stirring my imagination.
The anatomy lesson of Rembrandt
replaced by the anatomy lessons
of others, friends missing in these oppressive times.
And the friends too: replaced by reading
until snap! the optic nerve severs
somewhere in death's recesses.
A black tradition which Andersen (Never never forget!)
once strewed for us with rice, small beetles,
butcher shops filled with sunlight and dance.
In spite of all who wished it dead,
the spirit caresses our hair spread out below sea level
and so we awaken together again, the vertical ones,
present at something Rembrandt would never have painted
unless snap! the optic nerve...

Translated by Adam J. Sorkin and Angela Jianu

ELEGY III
[*Elegie III*]

We live a double life.
Here, the poem, the brutal dream, the lesson about verbs,
the rotary press of tomorrow and the day before.
Beyond the window, the ear of destiny
digging quietly in this autumn of cotton fluff.
Above everything, there exists
such a full-bellied equilibrium.
What madness, you tell yourself too late,
to survive happily articulating
the misfortunes of others!
But the ear of destiny
digs quietly in this autumn of cotton fluff,
while you find yourself fitting mysteries
into fiction for the blind:
Here, the hero, aloof,
happy on a green roof
murmurs along after the magi under the eyelids.
There, someone who abandoned you
is lonesomely rearranging his own past.
In the mind, in one part of the skull,
rakes and saints battle and quarrel.
In death's reciprocal angle,
liars and seers declaim and bustle.
Then you don't know a thing anymore: under the
                         eyelids ice clogs the shore
as the rotary press of tomorrow and the day before

swallows the poem, the table, the brutal dream,
the lesson about verbs.
Your hands are empty and hang heavily down.
Here, blanched with terror.
Beyond the window digging quietly
in this autumn of cotton fluff.

Translated by Adam J. Sorkin and Angela Jianu

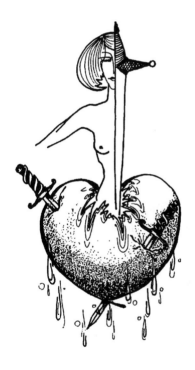

ELEGY VI
[*Elegie VI*]

Gone is the time
when my child's brow longed to be ablaze...

Gone is the restfulness of the poem
in which the hero died contentedly
on the golden parallels,
in which the dream dreaming on its own under the white skin
collected its ashes and mocked
such pliant anesthetics.

If I bind one word to another
I endure death
from a parched sound and an indefiniteness
that sets my hand on fire.

Gone from words is the pliant flesh
and the mud it stretches over
again wants us.

Translated by Adam J. Sorkin and Mia Nazarie

ELEGY VII
[*Elegie VII*]

Death's right here, among us,
and today she has suddenly grown younger.
"Hurry up! She's kind today!"
calls out a poet
whom necessity's empire
keeps at its gates
her feet frozen
in the snows of the last ice age.
Another poet,
from the midst of the empire,
tosses her some dry bread crusts left over
from our evening meal
and some energizing circumlocutions
from the time of the inquisition
that had chafed roughly at her ankles.

And so, poverty and death,
how they drag us after them
in immense nets of nerves...
Let's hurry up!
They're kind today!

Translated by Adam J. Sorkin and Mia Nazarie

ELEGY VIII
[*Elegie VIII*]

In love (of course) and obscured
in the carbide night of souls
death laughs and
sometimes she tells you
"How handsome you are as only in dreams"

and you feel so glad
you kiss her young arms

and then upon my breasts
oh, you no longer know what laughter is

"The dead no longer have mornings"
"The dead no longer have mornings"

she whispers

and you feel glad
you kiss her arms

and then upon my breasts
in the carbide night
it's the roar of derision in love
and obscured.

Translated by Adam J. Sorkin and Mia Nazarie

ELEGY IX
[*Elegie IX*]

Oh, the guilt and horror
before so many strangled truths!
Who will testify
about the crimes committed against us?
Today's simple words,
screwed into the only body
which can be given over to death,
will they, I wonder, make us be better?
I am not a moral being.
Yet can anyone at all remain alive and
unsullied, keep an integrity?
Sometimes, on tropical summer nights,
when I climb down the evolutionary ladder of this species,
I see and think with a single eye in my forehead
isolated and shattered.

Then I seem to hear curses and incantations
in a language in which we once used to dream.

Translated by Adam J. Sorkin and Angela Jianu

ELEGY XIV
[*Elegie XIV*]

You don't even know:
I've started all over from the beginning
the way morning cleans up insomnia's leftovers
and lays on your table a fiery existence.
I had the courage to work at the very root of the Evil
and exactly there open the workshops of
"the person who would draw nearer the self,"
who would conquer nothing but the truth,
one's own paltry tale.
Look at me!
I am a little uglier and a little absurd.
I laugh more and more seldom and I speak less and less,
much too late I again reach out this hand to you.

And you, do you too hear the blizzard already
                    sweeping away the future?

Translated by Adam J. Sorkin and Mia Nazarie

THE EARLY HOURS OF THE MORNING
[*În primele ore ale dimineții*]

They had been given just enough power
to understand they would never have any
(but that was much later).
They had been bought cheap:
cohorts of briars around their neck
and the road sprinkled with rice.
Upon their return
(but that too was later, much too late)
some had had their eyes put out
while others wore stones shackled to their ankles.

"This world in which we repeat ourselves stuttering"
"This world in which we repeat..."

They had been given just long enough a chain
to wish for a real guillotine.
In the morning,
the early hours of the morning.

Translated by Adam J. Sorkin and Mia Nazarie

CARMEN FIRAN
(1958-   )

Born on 29 November 1958 in Craiova, Carmen Firan is a young poet and writer who has taken an active role in promoting Romanian culture, both in the country and throughout the world. Although she completed a degree in mathematics at the University of Craiova, she has dedicated her life to writing, publishing her first volume of poems, *Iluzii pe cont propriu*, in 1981.

Her cultural activity displays a wide range of talents. Apart from poetry, for which she is best known, Carmen Firan's writings include plays, novels, and poems for children. A member of the Romanian Writers' Union, she has also worked as a columnist for one of the most important literary journals in the country, *România literară*, as well as publishing essays, articles, and poems in various other cultural journals throughout the country. Presently, she serves as the Executive Secretary of the Romanian Cultural Foundation where she is responsible for a wide range of programs, including organizing the publication of important works of Romanian literature, as well as several cultural magazines destined for Romanians living abroad. Her hard work and dedication are helping to make Romanian culture better known throughout the world.

Among the many young poets and writers working in Romania today, Carmen Firan stands out both for her dedicated efforts to promote Romanian culture generally, something quite admirable during this period of transition towards a democratic society in post-communist Romania, as well as for the unique sensibilities displayed in her poetry. For these reasons she ranks among the most important young Romanian women poets writing today.

Kurt W. Treptow

A POEM OF PURPLE LOVE
[poem de amor vinețiu]

The voices of night in carnal cadences
like the blind grope about the town
you think like a fish in the dark
you put on your armor over eyelids and fingers
without the five senses life can be beautiful
a photo maimed by the hand of a maestro

now you can love me
we are very much as if alone

their bodies are vibrating in walls
a price for art and quiet

we are very much as if alone
with an additional drama invented
telling you things about which
I know almost nothing
speaking about places that
I shall never see

the choir impotently hums
the first poem of purple love
that I have not ceased mystifying

the shape touches its body
it delays the return
although it recognizes the birth
the cry

the free pass into walls and behind bars
their breath is still a guarantee
for art and quiet

now you can love me
blindly, without thoughts
you can remove the newspapers, the ashes
and shake yourself clean
we are very much as if alone
turned into a wheel
of carnal cadences.

Translated by Andrei Bantaş

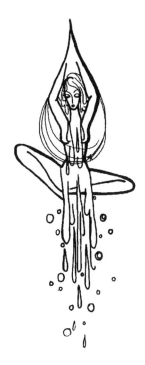

PARADOXES OF SLEEP
[*paradoxuri ale somnului*]

impossible, white illusions
out of which things have abandoned
both the shape and the soul
of he who lies flat between street and death

newspapers are no longer sold,
and even those we knew are but
paradoxes of sleep
of the mind through which
are panting the writing tools
and even the distorted real

one no longer sells illusions
the gate of the city is locked.

Translated by Andrei Bantaş

IN THE ABSENCE OF LOVE
[în lipsa dragostei]

the sea is sighing like a woman
and I can hear its breath
of a hunted man
nearby yellow flowers
wild stones
salt drops stinging my arms
two seagulls dart out of my eyes
and fly side by side
speaking to each other over water
like human beings
in the absence of love.

Translated by Andrei Bantaş

HIGH UNDERGROUND GALLERIES
[*subterane înalte*]

the poems displayed in the public square
hanged dolls
statues of rejected dreams

you are looking out from the window
at the ice blocks gliding on the lake
white coffins
toward the world without lust and blood

you are looking out from the window
at the city's edge
at its wounds as wet
as the muzzle of a rabid dog

you descend into high underground galleries
assailed by a winter of humiliation
that drags its knees through the mud
an old she-wolf
which with tears in its eyes
has devoured
its young ones

Translated by Andrei Bantaş

EVENTUALLY
[*în cele din urmă*]

poetry
a blue snake
stretches from one to the other
it breaks the shop window
it coils insiduously
around those driven
from the street into the house

it binds hands and learns to cry
the utterance at the service of power
don't throw the mantle of clouds
off my shoulders
remember
in the beginning was the word
in the last night
distorted

eventually
there remains poetry insinuated
like a blue snake
into the cup full of tears

Translated by Andrei Bantaş

CARMEN VERONICA STEICIUC
(1968-   )

The youngest of the poets presented in this anthology, Carmen Veronica Steiciuc represents the new young generation of Romanian writers, the beginning of whose careers coincide with the collapse of the communist dictatorship in Romania, the decisive event allowing a new freedom of expression in the country. While many have spoken of a cultural crisis in post-communist Romania, inspired young poets and writers such as Carmen Veronica Steiciuc quietly go about their writing and prove that Romanian literature is alive and well in this new era of freedom.

Born in Suceava in the northern part of Moldavia on 25 October 1968, Carmen Veronica Steiciuc is presently a student in computer science at the "Ştefan cel Mare" University in this historic Romanian city, once the medieval capital of the Romanian Principality of Moldavia. A direct descendant of the Romanian national poet, Mihai Eminescu, she made her literary debut in a regional literary magazine, *Pagini bucovinene*, in 1988. Since then her poems have appeared in many of the most important literary reviews in Romania, including *Familia, Tribuna, Vatra, Orizont,* and *Ateneu,* among others; she has also won numerous prizes throughout the country for her poems. In addition to her writing and her studies, she has been active working with orphan children in her native country.

Carmen Veronica Steiciuc is a fresh new voice in Romanian poetry and representative of a new generation of Romanian women poets. Her verse displays a remarkable sensitivity and depth of feeling, essential to poetic expression. Her forthcoming volume of poems should further demonstrate these characteristics and prove that she is among the finest young poets writing in Romania today.

Kurt W. Treptow

THE STREET WITH NUMBER TEN PLUS THREE
[strada cu număr de zece plus trei]

sometimes the sky is very close
and the angels

it's just at that moment you cross
the street or make lunch you
stop in front of a shop window or
browse through a book you raise the telephone receiver
wait in a railway station or turn on
the television six three the neighbors playing backgammon
the spider from the bathroom or merely the dog
scared from the last earthquake on
the stairs the bone one day
on the street with number ten plus three an
unhappy man is testing his wings on
the twenty-first floor it is the moment when...

but dear gentlemen you are unconscious
you don't see the car that just then
forgets to brake for reasons of insubordination
the knife that stops itself in the housewife's finger
the shop window that shatters at that very moment
the book with missing pages, the telephone without a tone
the deserted platform the three minutes to two train
will go tomorrow morning the horror

movie the scared dog the unhappy man from
the twenty first floor we need gentlemen
we truly need
an angel

Oh yes, yes sometimes the sky.

Translated by Kurt W. Treptow

YOU KNOW IT
[*doar ştii şi tu*]

motto: *"I'd like to sleep until September*
and then wake up being yours"

I just wanted to write about you on
that afternoon the pianist was playing
now and then the rain was tapping at my window
without fail was saying you're thinking of him
aren't you?

with wet palms
touching my temples since last monday nothing
has happened and things are
getting worse you should have
finished the book you are working on for
some months now you should have
answered Brenda

he doesn't know anything I said he's just
preparing his baggage, is gathering
his books and beloved things he's been
busy recently, surely
you know it

of course
said the rain and tossed in my room
the cold tears from the pocket near my heart

I called all morning long
but nobody answered I was gone for
the weekend will say on the phone
the voice later that afternoon
take care of yourself the night before that
I had a dream about you it was the
first time it's true I can't remember well
what happened when I
woke up I was crying it's
all I know

he will come again in September
said the rain and gathered in the eyelid's
ladle the memories from the summer holiday

till then there are many things to do
don't forget the promised translation and starting
next week the optional course
in English

----

on the table one visiting card that's all

now and then the rain stopped
at my window the pianist was playing
in that afternoon

I just wanted to write about you.

Translated by Kurt W. Treptow

OLIVETTI LETTERA 32
[*olivetti lettera 32*]

I found out that you are here and the thrill
passed through autumn's mirrors with all its reflections being
obscured the beast was screaming in
the box with letters the shadow of this poem
the roar of laughter started from the bow
specially prepared we had decided to
attack the first leaf the morning
was throwing itself in our bodies the words
were falling at the news stand there was
nobody and the hour stopped astonished
the gondolier had left when
our dreams with arms full of
shells were wandering throughout the nerves of memories
olivetti lettera 32 doesn't
type the word love the typewriter
mistakes freeze frame the gondolier
the leaf the mirrors are counting in reverse
(the thrill and I found out that you are here)

Translated by Kurt W. Treptow

THE CRYSTAL CHANDELIER
[*candelabrul de cristal*]

motto: *"My dreams are circular:*
they begin and end with you"

I came back to my room at 13:47
it seemed to me uninhabited that absence
the dreams were running scared
you'll never understand were calling
the spring's hidden in the house's eaves
you aren't but an illusion in the
cobweb the memories
were looking at me unhappy sometimes
I acknowledge their right but in that moment
it was hurting me your absence I was feeling even
the bullet that startled you
of course the angel shouldn't ever
have pressed the trigger and yet
from that poem your image
was starting to take shape with every word
read or maybe

I was watching you silently from the chair that
I used to call *mine* I was watching
every gesture every glance
you were telling me like always
a movie or an incident more
or less interesting the words
were remaining somewhere in air

suspended in a kind of crystal
chandelier uncertain space
a kind of

the voice was numbing my thoughts in a
colorless game pleasant as a matter of fact
I would have liked to have stopped maybe that writhe
of absurdity from the eye of the second to remain in this
                                                        way
with arms in the air explaining an episode
unmeaningful or merely

I asked myself several times if
that illusion could stop
the odd delirium we were predestined to
or if

he will believe you were shouting the summers from the
secret drawer the old envelope and your photograph
he will believe you in the moment when
the unbeing will imagine a supper for
the comedians who arrived in town
yesterday afternoon
the natives don't know much about
the masked ball organized in the memory of
your reflections next autumn when
you'll receive my greeting card you'll have to look at
the trees and ask them about their
previous existence the angel
will watch the memories that for
different reasons (maybe looking through

the book of poems you'll know more)
I left them in the care of the spider
last century

I knew that after a time you'll go
but I didn't want to believe it
I was watching every glance every gesture
everything seemed to be confused
you stood up
you asked something (I don't know what)
I was watching you leave and feeling
the weight of the absence that will follow you
were smiling all the time somewhere
on a wild island the wave
brought to shore a giant shell
why all these my God

I came back to my room at 13:47
I was feeling yet in the air your presence
on the walls painted in blue an uncertain
shape an indistinct outline
it might be a spider
said the voice descending from the crystal
chandelier it might be

Translated by Kurt W. Treptow

THE SNAKE TAMER
[*îmblînzitorul de şerpi*]

that tall guy and half absurd
reminded me of you in that special cut suit
for a special holiday it was
a party or I don't know what
does it matter the photographer said on the wedding
day smile please there! O.K.! it's
all right at the next change the dreams
might seem to be feasible
don't believe him the psycopath was shouting
don't believe him my cousins said
and blood brothers in that morning
the snake tamer asked me about you
as if by chance

clusters of unfinished images

later
that tall guy and half absurd
left slamming
the door behind him

Translated by Kurt W. Treptow

NOTE ON THE PRONUNCIATION OF ROMANIAN WORDS

This note is intended to give readers who are unfamiliar with the Romanian language some idea of the proper pronunciation of the Romanian words that appear in this book. Romanian orthography is almost entirely phonetical, a letter representing one and the same sound, in all positions, with few exceptions. Here are the letters of the Romanian alphabet and their pronunciation:

a - as a in half, but shorter.
ă - as er in father.
â - similar to e in morsel or u in sullen.
b - as b in baseball.
c - before consonants, the vowels a, ă, â, î, o, u and at the end of words, as c in cat. Before e and i, as ch in cherry.
d - as d in dog.
e - as e in pen.
f - as f in fire.
g - before consonants, the vowels a, ă, â, î, o, u and at the end of words, as g in got. Before e and i, as g in general.
h - as h in behind. In groups che, chi, ghe, ghi, it is mute, showing that c and g preserve their hard sound.
i - as ee in see.
î - similar to e in morsel or u in sullen. Same as â.
j - as s in measure.
k - as k in kite.
l - as l in like.
m - as m in mother.
n - as n in neither.
o - as o in comb.
p - as p in police.
r - similar to a rolled Scottish r.
s - as s in sand.
ş - as sh in ship.
t - as t in toil.
ţ - as ts in cats.
u - as u in glue.
v - as v in valley.
x - as x in excellent.
z - as z in zebra.